1

Surviving Marriage In The 21st Century: 13 Easy Tips That Can Help You Get to 20 Years and Beyond

By
Rufus & Jenny Triplett

Front & Back Cover Design: Rufus & Jenny Triplett

©2013 Dawah International, LLC, a Multimedia Company/Rufus & Jenny Triplett

Library of Congress Cataloged – In Publication Data

ISBN: 978-0615769387 Dawah International, LLC Publishing

Dawah International, LLC Publishing

PO Box 380

Powder Springs, GA 30127

678-233-8286

dawahinternationalllc@gmail.com

For Worldwide Distribution. Printed in the United States of America.

FOREWORD

Ebony Magazine's 'Couple of the Year' 2012 says Marriage is an Institution not a New Year's Resolution

Rufus and Jenny Triplett, whose marriage has survived 23 plus years, have been selected by Ebony Magazine as Couple of the Year for 2012. Their plain and simple approach to marriage and the commitment needed in order to sustain it has resonated through their marriage tips and relationship advice given to newlyweds, engaged couples, veteran couples and dating couples alike as well as the editors of Ebony Magazine. Their individual male and female perspectives are different as to what makes a marriage work but they both acknowledge communication as the greatest survival tip.

They have a wealth of tips to share and cover various aspects of marriage. As they share 13 main tips in this books as well as a plethora of other short tidbits, here is a couple to get you warmed to their vibe.

Here is one of Jenny's Favorites:

- **Marriage is a Marathon Not a Sprint** – Get into the mindset that there are going to be hurdles just as there are in life. Tackle them with patience, love and understanding. Keep an even stride. Slow and steady wins the race.

Here is one of Rufus' Favorites:

- **Marriage is a Super Fragile – Handle it with Care** – Making a decision to get married was not a decision that was made on a whim. Treat your marriage as you would a newborn baby, with care. Learn and grow with it as it grows and brings you together.

DEDICATION

First & foremost we would like to bear witness to the Oneness of God and thank HIM for Blessing us and keeping us together for all of these years and seeing us through the hard times when our marriage could have very easily folded. We would also like to thank HIM for keeping us from strangling one another while trying to put this book together. Yall have no idea.

Special Words

Please note that we do not condone domestic violence. If anyone is in a relationship where they are being abused, please get help. These tips are to help strengthen marriages and for healthier relationships. Abuse, in any form – mental, verbal, spiritual, sexual and physical, is truly disliked by the both of us.

mar·riage

/'marij/

Noun
1. The formal union of a man and a woman, typically recognized by law, by which they become husband and wife.
2. A relationship between married people or the period for which it lasts.

Marriage
Marriage is a social union or legal contract between people called spouses that establishes rights and obligations between the spouses, between the spouses and their children, and between the spouses and their in-laws. Wikipedia

surviving present participle of *sur·vive* **(Verb)**

Verb
1. Continue to live or exist, esp. in spite of danger or hardship.
2. Continue to live or exist in spite of (an accident or ordeal).

INTRODUCTION

This book stemmed from an idea of giving marriage advice to various people after years of being asked "how do you make it work" or that we "make it look easy." During the course of 2011 & 2012, numerous #Marriagetips were shared on twitter which helped to create the buzz for this book and we would like to share them with you all in rewind.

Here are several to get you started and there will be more at intermission (because we all need a breather) and at the end. Please feel free to share these tips with anyone you think may benefit. Now that does not mean to bootleg the book or take our words as your own…it just means to share what you have learned and how these tips may have been of benefit to you. Also, feel free to read them again and again when you feel as if you have hit a wall and can't go any further.

MARRIAGE TIPS from Twitter

marriage takes two commitments…#marriagetip

marriage is an institution not a new year's resolution #marriagetip

20 plus years of marriage is not a fluke #marragetip

The saying goes…it's cheaper her…a fool and his money is soon departed. #marriagetip

Get Married…best #marriagetip for 2012 or any year

When you treat your woman like @BarackObama…she will glow like @MichelleObama…#marriagetip

It's funny how when your eyes are open to a situation you can see crystal clear. Clean your glasses. #marriagetip

#onething you need to know about surviving marriage is that you shouldn't push buttons to create hurt #marriagetip

Shower your spouse with love everyday...#marriagetip

if you really want to get married and do the right thing it does not take years...#marriagetip

"Courtship brings out the best. Marriage brings out the rest." #marriagetip

20 years at anything makes you an expert...:-)#marriagetip

Last time we checked marriage made you honorable. If you're "just together" there is not much honor in that. #marriagetip

marriage will never be dead. Backward thinking people who like to change the thoughts and perceptions of society are making this up #marriagetip

TRUST is a big word in relationships. #marriagetip

Marriage is a Marathon not a Sprint - #MarriageTip

Treat your spouse right and everything else will fall in line - #marriagetip

We never know what goes on behind closed doors. Love in a marriage is a love that comes from within #marriagetip

Love is a verb #marriagetip

When you can sit in a room with your spouse & enjoy tv without convo but just looks with meaning, you know you are connected. #marriagetip

#marriagetip it is better to marry than flaunt fornication

Believe it or not, someone has to be the leader in a Marriage.

#marriagetip

#Marriagetip Marriage is about more than the ring and the bling

Nobody has to always be right. If you ever hear my way or the highway you need to be on the next thing smoking. #marriagetip

Make your Marriage a happy home #marriagetip

Money arguments are bound to happen when two are spending like two instead of one. #marriagetip?

It's never too late to get married #marriagetip

A king knows how to treat his queen. #marriagetip

A good apology has three parts: 1 I'm sorry. 2 It's my fault. 3 What can I do to make it right? A good husband will know this. #marriagetip

Compromising with someone you are not married to is like going to work and not getting a paycheck. You don't owe them anything #marriagetip

Good Times and Bad Times...they're going to happen. Stick together and work it out...with peace. #marriagetip

There doesn't always have to be a reason to do something for your spouse. Sometimes do it...just because...#marriagetip

FYI: When a wife says "come here" she doesn't mean 20 questions later. #marriagetip

To further the reach of the tips, we changed the #hashtag from #Marriagetip to #Marriagetips...and here ya go...

#marriagetips if your friends cannot respect your marriage it's time to find new friends

beware of the folks who tell you not to get married in the first place. Consider the source. #marriagetips

#5myths about marriage -- myth 1: People don't value marriage the way they used to

#marriagetips Happy Wife, Happy Life, Happy Strife

#marriagetips the marriages or lack of marriages on TV does not have to be a reflection of your marriage

#marriagetips marriage after kids enhances 20 fold

#marriagetips if you spend more time with your friends than you do with your spouse that is who you will eventually end up with

#marriagetips if you are not having makeup sex after a disagreement you are missing out on one of the best parts of marriage

Please note the informal formatting of the tips…hey…it's Twitter…140 characters…okaaay.

Can we get some RT's (retweets…☺)

TABLE OF CONTENTS

TIP 1 – Put God First

God must be a central component of your marriage. Everyone has their own relationship with God, if you believe, and the majority of marriage ceremonies are performed in some type of religious institution with a presiding religious notary.

Thus, we can say that the belief in a higher power for guidance is what should be your go to when you are on the ropes with how to handle things in your marriage. If both parties are seeking to please God and pray for a lasting and sustaining marriage, then HE should be remembered when things are going bad AND when things are going well.

After all, Marriage is half of your faith.

Tip 1 Discussion:

Jenny: Our first tip is to put God first dear. What would you have to say in regards to marriages and God.

Rufus: First I would have to say that marriage would not exist if HE did not create it. HE created something for us that we didn't know would be good for us. Marriage is a union between a man and a wife but it has to be a covenant with God as well. I'm saying God has to come first.

Jenny: Okay, so what do you say to the people who don't have God to go to or who don't believe?

Rufus: God has to be a part of that union between a man and his wife. Ya betta get at HIM.

Jenny: So you say maybe this isn't for those people who don't believe?

Rufus: Marriage is a commitment and when you struggle with that commitment there has to be a higher power to consult for resolution.

Jenny: So, that wouldn't be my mother or your mother or your boys or my girls?

Rufus: Shoot no. Somebody gone learn today.

TIP 2 – Respect Your Vows (Be Committed – For Better or For Worse)

Marriage is Forever – For Better or for Worse, For Richer or For Poorer, In Sickness and Health – Til Death Do Us Part. Respect Your Vows.

We are no longer living in the times of the 1960's where couples married young. It was a goal of those North, South, East and West to marry like June and Ward Cleaver.

Generation X started to stray away from the foundation of marriage. The statists of teen pregnancy and single parents, more so single mothers and baby daddies started to increase. Sexual freedoms became abundantly apparent. All of the things that were being done in the dark were coming to the light.

The commitment of marriage is more than a formatted or fermented idea in your head. The commitment to stay with someone while forsaking all others all of the rest of the days of your lives is an idea that must resonate with your soul.

Tip 2 Discussion:

Jenny: Respect your vows, be committed for better or for worse that's our second tip dear. What do you have to say to that?

Rufus: Respect me woman.

Jenny: What about giving me respect and you shall receive it back once you obey me.

Rufus: Why do we keep bringing up obey?

Jenny: Because it's one of those words that is controversial. In most vows, especially the traditional ones, spoken in front of God, it says to love, honor and obey. I believe that goes both ways.

Rufus: If that goes both ways, then why don't you obey me when I ask you to get out and pump some gas? Or turn the TV to something I want to watch? It seems like obey only works for you...yes dear.

Jenny: You darn skippy. That's why ours works so well. Marriage is forever. Remember what you asked me right before we got married? You asked me "are you sure" because you said when you get married it's forever. I was sure because I knew you were going to obey me.

Rufus: Obey you? I wanted to be sure that you weren't playing around and that you would respect the part of till death do us part. I wanted to let you know that I wasn't playing games so if you were playing games you could get to stepping.

Jenny: Oh, now you know I was raised to be independent and would have had no problem stepping off but I was committed to getting married even though we had what some would call irreconcilable differences.

Rufus: Oh, why didn't I know about them, did you reconcile them?

Jenny: You knew about them and WE reconciled them. WE came to some resolve on whatever issues we had because we knew we were about making our marriage work. We didn't want our marriage to be a drive-by marriage. We had already seen enough of those and odds were definitely against us.

Rufus: I was going make it work regardless. I was in it to win it.

Jenny: I, marriage is we. Glad you were married to yourself.

Rufus: Ok, why you trying to be so hard…

TIP 3 – Don't Try to Change the Person You Married

Don't Try to Mold or Change the Person You Fell in Love with
Remember when you choose to spend the rest of your life with someone that it is that person at that time to which you are agreeing. Don't try to change the little quirks that one has or make them someone that they are not because they will not like it and eventually you won't either.

Tip 3 Discussion:

Jenny: Our third tip is don't try to change the person you marry or the person you fell in love with. Can't wait to hear what you have to say about that one dear.

Rufus: Leave me be woman.

Jenny: Look, I'm just asking you what you have to say about folks trying to change other folks.

Rufus: The person you love has bad habits as we all have bad habits.

Jenny: Are you saying I have bad habits? Please be clear as to what you are saying? IF, and I do mean IF I have any bad habits, you have embraced those bad habits and come to love them. Just saying.

Rufus: Oh, you want those skeletons to fall out of the closet and chase you around the room. I'm not going to beat you up about them. I'm just going to say that people fall in love with people with habits or things about them that they would like to change.

Jenny: Yeah, you know like the quirky little faces that you use to make that I thought was cute 20 years ago and now when you make them they get on my nerves...like those habits dear? But I'm not going to try to change you.

Rufus: The only person you can change is yourself. People try to change people but it does not work.

Jenny: Oh, it's things that everybody needs to change in any relationship, but it's up to that person to do it. Work on self. Maybe you married someone who wasn't the best dresser and now after marriage you want to give them a makeover. They loved to wear tennis shoes or flip-flops and all of a sudden you want them wearing Stacy Adams and Gucci. You know darn well that is not the person that you fell in love with.

Rufus: What's Gucci got to do with it?

Jenny: What's love got to do with it?

Rufus: Love should have brought you home.

Jenny: Gucci is looked at as being fashionable and maybe you want to make that person over to a higher standard. It happens. Love keeps me home dear…

Rufus: Change is for yourself. I'll work on change for me and hopefully the relationship matures where the other person sees their flaws and maybe they'll make changes too.

Jenny: Okay, changing someone and telling someone how you feel about their flaws is two different things. Don't stop the communication.

Rufus: It's not what you say it's how you say it.

Jenny: I'm only going to mention something to you, once, twice…maybe three times, but ultimately it's up to you to change it.

Rufus: What you have to do is you have to turn that mirror around and reflect on self. I believe in working on getting self together.

Jenny: You wanna hold my mirror dear?

Rufus: I said leave me be woman.

TIP 4 – Have Open Communication

Have Open Communication – Be willing to talk about anything and everything. Humor your partner for what they want to know. Sharing is bonding.

Tip 4 Discussion:

Jenny: Oh great, now we get to talk about communication. It's definitely in the top 5 of tips but a vital part of surviving marriages. Now what's on your mind about this tip dear?

Rufus: I'm always open for discussions. You gotta be open. You gotta be able to receive what somebody has to say. So do be open. Now where's my dinner?

Jenny: Dinner? We are writing a book dear. Dinner can wait or you can let your fingers do the walking and order some takeout. So do you think tone is important?

Rufus: It ain't got nothing to do with tone it's just being open.

Jenny: There is a proper way to communicate. So if I come yelling at you and you know I'm upset, we're going to have a nice discussion...right?

Rufus: Yelling at who? Ok, then tone is everything. What I know is going to happen is that nice discussion may not be so nice. It's all about the way you come at me.

Jenny: So what are you saying? It is about tone.

Rufus: No, that's a miscommunication. Yelling is not love.

Jenny: But yelling shows passion and love is passionate.

Rufus: Yell at me and see what you get.

Jenny: What advice would you give to the people who don't have good communication in a relationship?

Rufus: Just to talk. Talk and say what's on your mind.

Jenny: Okay, we know a lot of people that go to marriage counselors because they don't have good communication. What they have is a failure to communicate.

Rufus: The best of us are talkers. The best way to start is just to start talking.

Jenny: No dear, YOU are a talker. Communication is a 2 way street. You have to be open to receiving (hearing and understanding) as well as open to talking.

Rufus: Well what we have here is a failure to communicate. Open it up…breathe.

Jenny: What does breathing have to do with it?

Rufus: Take a breath and then say what's on your mind. Breathe.

Jenny: I do believe in taking pauses. Pause, take a time out and don't have a discussion when you're angry because it's not a discussion when you're angry. It's called arguing. Arguing can be toxic. But that's another book.

Rufus: Time out? This ain't kindergarten. This some grown folks stuff here.

TIP 5 – Treat Your Marriage Like A Job

Marriage is hard work. Put in all of the effort that you would as if you were climbing the corporate ladder. Work through difficulties, tolerate pet peeves, work overtime when needed, plan meetings to discuss job description and direction and take time for self when needed.

Make sure that when it is time for compensation, everything is done in a fair and just manner. No one should ever be unhappy being married to the boss.

"Act like your marriage is a job. Treat it as if you were climbing the corporate ladder. Address your challenges, work overtime when needed, and plan meetings to discuss how you're doing. It's the most important gig you'll ever have!"

—*Jenny and Rufus Triplett, together since they were 16*

TIP 6 – Discuss Money or Money Will Disgust You

It is not uncommon for couples to divorce over money issues. Some of the biggest arguments in marriages are about money, not enough, not spending it incorrectly and sometimes too much money can cause marital friction. Make sure that you are discussing all money matters and making major decisions together.

Impulse buying and splurging are not always wise decisions when the mortgage is due and the lights are about to be turned off for non-payment. Don't place blame on one another for their spending habits. Put the issues on the table and work it out with Monopoly money.

Tip 6 - As Printed in Reuters & Fox Business – Marriage & Money – June 2012

YOUR MONEY-How couples sabotage their finances

Minor money differences can be overcome as long as you have the basics covered: You have your daily needs met, you're bringing in more than you're paying out, and you're able to build a nest egg for the future. But once overspending and debt enter the picture, all bets are off.

"I was always a black-belt shopper, and hated to miss a sale," says Jenny Triplett, an entrepreneur in Powder Springs, Georgia, who's been married to husband Rufus Triplett for 22 years. "I'd have bags full of new clothes in the closet, and only bring them out one piece at a time. But eventually we came to a compromise, and I got my spending under control."

That's exactly the right template for resolving money disputes, planners advise. Even with differing money styles, if both partners take strides toward the middle and agree on broad outlines of a budget, it could prevent countless disputes.

TIP 7 – Don't Keep Secrets

The quickest way to destroy a relationship is to have a spouse find out about a secret. Depending on how major the secret is, there will be a discussion or there will be fireworks. Immediately, TRUST has left the building.

When you commit to a life together, that is a total commitment. Full disclosure is necessary. Internal third degrees and background checks are not fun, for either party.

Tip 7 Discussion:

Jenny: Love this tip! Don't keep secrets. That's something you can enlighten the folks on right dear?

Rufus: I don't do secrets.

Jenny: You don't keep secrets from me…right?

Rufus: *(sanging –almost like Babyface) Girl I'm never keeping secrets and I'm never telling lies*

Jenny: Liar.

Rufus: What?

Jenny: Is there anything you want to tell me?

Rufus: Like my mama say you lost your everlasting mind…calling me a liar.

Jenny: Well, I'm communicating in my own way. I think there's something that you need to tell me.

Rufus: You done lost your marbles.

Jenny: Well, I'll say it again, we don't have any secrets do we dear?

Rufus: I don't do groups. (*American Idol reference*)

Jenny: Don't change the subject. You know that secret bank account you have.

Rufus: First of all, I don't have a secret bank account. You know about that account.

Jenny: I know about everything. Let's not forget who gets all the mail around here. Don't get it twisted. I was just checking to see if

30

there was some MORE I needed to know before the "til death do us part" part comes into play.

Rufus: All I'm saying is I don't do secrets.

Jenny: No one should do secrets – secret accounts, secret affairs, secret outings, none of it. Having secrets are definitely relationship killers. Never, never keep secrets in a relationship and never tell lies.

Rufus: Anywho

Jenny: Laaawd I need a break. That's no secret.

INTERMISSION

Sooo…how are you liking the book so far? Hopefully it's everything you expected it to be. Everyone needs a break. Yeah, we know it's only a few pages, a real page turner and you will probably finish it at one setting, but hey, we needed a break while writing it so enjoy the music… we mean the tips…

MORE MARRIAGE TIPS from Twitter

#marriagetips Connect with your mate daily. It makes you in tune with their needs.

Real marriages are not a Woody Allen movie. Trials and tribulations are not over in two hours. #marriagetips

Love conquers all... True love #marriagetips

How deep is your love? #marriagetips

Sex starts outside the bedroom. Maybe there is a lack of connection in the overall marriage besides in the sex... #marriagetips

Don't try to change the person you married. It is the person in which you fell in love. You are both individuals with feelings #marriagetips

No one has to be happy with your mate but you. If you & your mate make each other happy then everyone else is irrelevant. #marriagetips

How long can you be a fiancé?? Long engagements and short #marriages. We must have missed the memo. #marriagetips

three words for long marriages... Fab-u-Lous! #marriagetips

Marriage is a relationship in which one person is always right and the other is the husband. #marriagetips

We still date after 22 years and sometimes we go Dutch... Lol #marriagetips

respect it, work at it, nurture it #marriagetips

Marriage is super fragile #marriagetips

22+ years of marriage has not stopped our sex life. Not even a hysterectomy. The brain is the most sexual muscle #marriagetips

secrets and lies destroys marriages #marriagetips

Now you will see the addition of the #hashtag #maritalbliss as we wanted to express the good about marriage since you are always hearing the bad about marriage

MORE MARRIAGE TIPS from Twitter

Happily Ever Afters are not just for Disney Movies. There are happy Marriages just like the fairytales. Real life Cinderella's. #maritalbliss

What's understood in marriages does not have to be explained. #marriagetips #maritalbliss

Shopping is understood lol #marriagetips #maritalbliss

Don't let little disagreements turn into huge blowouts. There can be resolve without discord. #marriagetips #maritalbliss

Marriage does not have to be a prison. #marriagetips #maritalbliss

One piece of paper I never mind producing for the ins company - our Marriage License. A piece of paper with a lot of power. #marriagetips

Marriage is an institution #marriagetips

Being married 22+ years means we always have a +1 and a travel buddy. The party can be just with the two of us. #marriagetips #maritalbliss

If you carry the bricks from your past relationship to the new one, you will build the same house. #marriagetips

#marriagetips Whenever you can, clean the kitchen together. Every 1loves to eat but no one like to clean. Share the responsibility. Rewarding

Marriages are meant to last a lifetime. When they don't all the world suffers. #marriagetips

#marriagetip whoever is driving controls the radio. Saves a lot of arguments. #maritalbliss

Asking and Nagging are two separate and distinct words. #marriagetips #maritalbliss

marriage is better than fornication #marriagetips

#marriagetips don't sweat the small stuff. It turns into big stuff.

Don't let little disagreements turn into huge blowouts. There can be resolve without discord. #marriagetips #maritalbliss

I truly am blessed with my husband. Man of the year ever year. #marriagetips #maritalbliss

Some of the most successful marriages are those where couples have been BFF's. Love being attached. #maritalbliss #marriagetips

marriage is not an excuse to let yourself go #marriagetips

When your husband says don't worry about dinner out of the b two days in a row you know you married the best man ever! #marriagetip

Marriage is special #marriagetips

One can give without loving but one cannot love without giving. #marriagetip

To have a good marriage, you must take care of YOURSELF. #marriagetips

Love and adore your husband #marriagetips

A happily married man is one who understands every word that his wife didn't say. If you are tuned in, you understand. #marriagetips

Two individuals have to be emotionally well to be happily married #marriagetips

WE Inspire, Innovate & Ignite thinking regarding marriage #marriagetips

Keep your marriage first! #marriagetips

Never keep secrets.... #marriagetips

The military is hard on marriages, but so is prison. Anyone who is surviving. We salute you. #marriagetips

Marriage is when a man and woman become as one #marriagetips

TIP 8 – Be Forgiving and Don't Sweat the Small Stuff

No matter how long you've been married, there is always something that is going to come up to which you is going to rub you the wrong way. The key is not to let it turn into a big deal . Talk about it, don't' let it fester and move on.

For example, being loud and outspoken should not be a deal breaker in a marriage. Normally one person is more outspoken than the other. Talk about the proper times in which to be verbose and the times in which to use the inside voice and not the outside voice.

Pressing the toothpaste from the middle or from the end should not be a deal breaker in a marriage. It's small stuff. Discuss to do it one way or the other or buy two tubes of toothpaste, his and hers.

Similar discussions about sorting the clothes, when to fill up the car with gas and if the potatoes should go in the refrigerator or the pantry should not be deal breakers in a marriage. These are small items. Seriously, don't sweat it.

Tip 8 Discussion:

Narrated by Jenny

Gonna tell you a little story about the small stuff. This is one of our favorite stories from the early years of our marriage. Never having lived together we had to learn each other's ways and what was of importance to one another. Needless to say, buying groceries for the first time as a married couple was a straight up trip.

We came from two different backgrounds and lived different lives with different diets. I was a fruit person and he was a pack of cookies person – the whole pack. I was a Cheerios and Cornflakes type of gal while he was Cocoa Crisps and Captain Crunch.

Well, we were young and broke, or rather on a budget, so there had to be some decisions made, sometimes right there in the grocery store. We had to agree on what we were going to eat without breaking the bank. The more we shopped the more we realized that we had to agree on several items that were household items and were to be shared. From the type of toothpaste, soap and toilet paper that we used to the type of dish liquid, laundry detergent and orange juice to buy, it was all different. And whether or not to buy a TV Guide almost became a weekly discussion. I loved any type of TV Guide and not having one, before the digital era of smart phones and internet, made me feel like I was missing something.

These were small differences, that we never thought about before marriage, that could have turned into major problems if we had let them. They were not even close to being deal breakers or irreconcilable. You learn how to resolve things as you grow and mature.

Since we lived off of military pay, we decided that on the 1st we would buy Captain Crunch and on the 15th we would buy Cheerios. Simple. It was just the two of us and cereal lasts if you don't eat the whole box in a day. The other items worked themselves out along the way.

Small problems with simple resolutions. Don't sweat them.

TIP 9 – Speak Kind Words

There is an old joke that refers to the wife as the "old ball and chain." Then there's the old joke that refers to the man who feels he has "married his mother." In the new millennium where marriage is being devalued less and less as an institution, the Wall Street Journal is shedding light on the Nagging Spouse Syndrome.

Women are stereotyped as nags but only to men who feel that they do not need micromanaging. Men, on the other hand, having the same mannerisms would be considered controlling. Numerous marriages are dissolved for irreconcilable differences. Maybe those are the code words for nagging or controlling.

Nagging—the interaction in which one person repeatedly makes a request, the other person repeatedly ignores it and both become increasingly annoyed—is an issue every couple will grapple with at some point. While the word itself can provoke chuckles and eye-rolling, the dynamic can potentially be as dangerous to a marriage as adultery or bad finances. We say it is exactly the type of toxic communication that can eventually sink a relationship.

Tip 9 (GRAPHIC)

accomplished   admirable   amazing
bright   amusing
articulate   benevolent   charismatic
charming   cheerful
brilliant   captivating
compassionate   congenial   constant   courageous
entertaining   delightful   disciplined   engaging
dedicated   incredible   fearless   caring
ingenious   kindhearted
inspiring   motivating
passionate
intelligent   respectful
sensational   sincere   stunning   trustful
understanding   unique   original   marvelous
powerful   remarkable   resourceful   loyal
pleasing   gracious   honorable
genuine
generous   fascinating   extraordinary

TIP 10 – Don't Believe Marriage is Perfect

NO marriage is perfect. Period.

Tip 10 Discussion:

(written by Jenny and published in the December 2012 Issue of Delux Magazine)

The Bling in Your Ring Does Not Mean a Thing

Eight has always been a nice round number. It is even prettier when placed before karat and after the word priceless. Everyone knows that a priceless eight-karat ring or any ring larger than a golf ball is guarantees of a successful marriage. Ask yourself what would be the problem? Any girl would be happy to have the ring of Kim Kardashian's dreams. That means 20.5 karats of happiness, right?

A great ring means that the future husband wants to show his future wife that he can shower here with the finer things in life. But hold the baguette, has anyone talked about who's going to do the dishes or the laundry? What about nights out with the boys' or the girls'? Or even who has control of the remote? It's the small things, weighing more than the price of a karat, that gives the marriage substance and what matters most.

I would be remiss not to give the totally distracted couples, who are more worried about the dress and the gifts for the bridal and groom's parties, some words of wisdom. For the sake of stronger marriages and the voice of reason within the midst of confusion, here goes what is hopefully considered clarity.

Marriage is a union between two individuals. It is where "me" becomes "we." Don't get blinded by pomp and circumstance. When the wedding planner writes the Thank You note and the honeymoon pictures are no longer receiving comments on Facebook, the marathon has already started. The path to Happily Ever After sets in and the work begins.

Don't try to change the person you married. That is whom you fell in love and to whom you said I Do. Work together to make all that glitter, solid gold.

TIP 11 – Learn How to Agree to Disagree

Marriages do not have to end with irreconcilable differences if the differences are small enough to be resolved. Younger marriages moreso than older marriages are going to have huge disagreements about what to watch on TV, to yard work, to raising the kids to what's for dinner.

Just because you are married does not mean that you are going to agree with everything your partner says. Learn how to disagree effectively by making and maintaining your point as well as keeping it lighthearted where you don't have to go to be angry.

Tip 11 Discussion:

As Printed in NY Magazine/The Cut 1/13

Doughnuts and OCD

"She brings Dunkin' Donuts in the house!" Rufus exclaims. "Cook me vegetables!"

"A forty-plus-year-old should have willpower!" Jenny playfully replies in mock anger. "I'm not cooking!"

"After twenty-plus years of marriage," she continues, "I can't say, 'Look, dear, you need to work out.' We have to keep it lighthearted. We both know what we need to do." She weighs herself daily, which Rufus considers "OCD."

"I tell him I see rolls, and he tells me to stop looking," Jenny notes. "If he loses his chest, I'll still love my husband."

His advice to young couples: "No harsh words." Her advice: "Don't expect to stay the same."

Hear more about Learning How to Agree to Disagree in our Bonus Audio Tips.

TIP 12 – Keep Outside Influence to a Minimum

Don't Put Others Before Your Spouse – Once you marry you become as one. No one should be more important than the relationship between you and your spouse. Outsiders such as friends, parents, co-workers, siblings and other relatives may think differently but in order to keep your relationship intact, respect your spouse.

Tip 12 Discussion:

Jenny: Outside influences, boy do we know all about them. I married into a huge family. It got interesting really quick. There were a lot of outsiders in our marriage when we first got married.

Rufus: I don't do outsiders.

Jenny: You did do outsiders. You don't remember we had a house full of people? It interrupted our marriage. That's what outside influences. Sometimes they are not good.

Rufus: Nobody interrupted my marriage.

Jenny: What about your friends? *(singing TLC's song What About Your Friends)*

Rufus: This ain't no TLC concert.

Jenny: Should friends have any type of influence on your marriage?

Rufus: Friends ain't got no influence on this marriage but we know some people who tell their friends everything about their marriage. Wrong answer.

Jenny: Friend should be there when you need them but they should butt out of your business.

Rufus: When it comes to me and my spouse, they definitely should. They only do what you allow them to do anyway.

Jenny: What about sharing of information about your marriage with your friends?

Rufus: What do you mean? Me, personally? I'm not sharing anything, not even with my mother.

Jenny: You like to talk so I'm having a hard time believing that. Let's just say you share some things and that's ok. But you know what to share and what not to share. And the same with me and my family. That is the respect that we have for one another.

Rufus: You should definitely be sharing with family members if somebody is abusing you or you fear for your life.

Jenny: Okay we're not talking about abusive relationships here, we're just talking about relationships in general, the ones that are a little less dysfunctional, and how much to involve friends and family. Toxic relationships will have to be another book.

Rufus: I'm talking about it all and once again you shouldn't let outsiders, and that includes co-workers, influence you to a point. It depends, you know. They shouldn't come between a man and his wife if there is no abuse happening.

TIP 13 – Become Best Friends

Some of the longest lasting and happiest marriages have survived because the couple were the best of friends and did just about everything together.

There is a great feeling to be married to a person with whom you can laugh, cry, shop, travel, share your emotions, raise a family and make lifelong memories.

Tip 13 Discussion:

Jenny: It's our last tip dear so make it good. How do couples become best friends, BFF's as they call them?

Rufus: Stay out the way. Move, stay out the way... get out the way.

Jenny: Move, get out the way? How did we become best friends if I stayed out your way?

Rufus: Stay out of my way, out of my business, away from my business and we cool.

Jenny: You're not answering the question. It's about to be time for me to change my communication techniques to help you better understand. How did we become best friends and what do couples need to know about how it can help them?

Rufus: I don't know, it just happened. I know I'm supposed to know but we've been married so long it seems as if we have always been the best of friends. If they incorporate everything that we have talked about, all the tips that we have given, it should happen for them.

Jenny: You're getting old dear. I say that lovingly. You have to agree that your BFF, your best friend makes you feel good; feel good about yourself and about life.

Rufus: I said if I didn't make you my best friend I was going to be in trouble. Anyway, that's how we have we become best friends. So instead of taking my boy to the game I starting taking my wife to the game.

Jenny: Is there a problem with taking me to the game? It's a lot of women that like sports and I just happened to be one of them. But this isn't for everyone because if husbands would rather go with friends because their wives don't like sports then that's ok too.

Rufus: Exactly, but you know if you rather hang out with your boy instead of hanging out with your spouse then I see that as a problem.

Jenny: You can go and hang out with me at the spa and it's all good. Husbands hang out at spas all the time.

Rufus: I don't do spas.

Jenny: You don't do massages but you do do spas. There's nothing wrong with you coming to hang out while I get my massages. You normally find something to eat. It's all good.

Rufus: What I'm saying is that the bottom line is if you hang around somebody more than you hang around your spouse you're going to end up with them.

Jenny: Would you say we were best friends when we first got married?

Rufus: Huh?

Jenny: Now you're getting selective hearing. Would you say we were best friends when we first got married?

Rufus: Ah… ah..yeah

Jenny: You're stuttering dear.

Rufus: Nah, I am answering the question.

Jenny: Anything else for the couples… anything else dear?

Rufus: Yeah be safe.

Jenny: Safe? Safe from what?

Rufus: Safe from self. Self is your worst enemy.

Well…there ya have it. That's some of the best darn advice we can give to those who want to make it work. Can it help you? Sure. If you work on your marriage and believe in forever, yes it can. Will it help you? That is totally up to the two parties involved in the struggle. Either you are willing to survive or you're not. You can lead a horse to water but you can't make them drink. Here's hoping the Kool-Aid was so sweet, you'll come back for seconds. This is Jenny from the block and I'm dropping the mic.

MARRIAGE TIPS for the Road...

Become the Best of Friends BFF's. It helps the marriage. #survivingmarriage

TRUST is give and get. You have to give it in order to get it. #survivingmarriage

Do not embarrass your spouse in front of others #survivingmarriage

Never neglect your spouse/family for your business. #survivingmarriage

More marriages would thrive if more people realized that the best usually comes after the worst.

Never shoot daggers at your spouse as the scars may never heal. #survivingmarriage

It's take two people putting in the work in order to make it to 20 years of marriage and beyond. #survivingmarriage

Marriage is a commitment and should only be between two people #survivingmarriage

#SurvivingMarriage is blending like good coffee. The best of times is like cream that rises to the top

#SurvivingMarriage has its rewards and comes with great celebrations.

#SurvivingMarriage - The past is where you learned the lesson. The future is where you apply the lesson. Don't give up in the middle!"

Knowing what buttons of your spouse's not to push can help you get to the golden years. #survivingmarriage

Boost your mate in public and private. Let your happiness emanate daily. #survivingmarriage

Honor your vows of MARRIAGE as they did not include being shallow. #survivingmarriage

It takes a few minutes to say "I DO" but several years to make it true. #survivingmarriage

Knowing when to say I'm sorry will get you closer to 20+years if marriage. #survivingmarriage

Knowing how to express love will help you love longer.#survivingmarriage

One of the best ways to keep a marriage is to be faithful. #survivingmarriage

Save yourself from Divorce Court by listening to the nonverbal communication. #survivingmarriage

Having to check cell phones for secrets is a breakdown in trust. It takes communication to strengthen it. #survivingmarriage

In sickness and in health spouses should be a comfort for one another. #survivingmarriage

Effective Communication starts early in a marriage. It's a major key to #survivingmarriage

Marriage can be beautiful but nobody said it would be perfect. #survivingmarriage

Good Marriages don't just happen. It's about pulling up your bootstraps and doing the work. #survivingmarriage

You have to BE married to survive a marriage. #survivingmarriage

#SurvivingMarriage...some of the best years of marriage are the latter years. Hold on as they can be golden.

#SurvivingMarriage...it takes forgiveness

Tripism - Magical Moments are Created Together. Create the right ones or you may create one that ends on Divorce Court #survivingmarriage

Tripism - Two fun-loving people will always find the "fun" in everything they do. #survivingmarriage

A Match Only Heaven Could Make

The year was 1985, the city was Flint, and the weather was cold. Me and my best friend Val had hooked up with READY FOR THE WORLD and became friends with their families. One night, while over one of their homes, Rufus Triplett, Jr. walks thru the door. The only attention I paid to him was his name. I couldn't stop laughing. I didn't think anyone had a name like that in those days. It was so old fashioned. He denies that he was checking me out, but he was. His cousin, Swain, thought we we're destined to be together so he started to play matchmaker. We saw each other on a couple of occasions but we never really talked. I was cool with the majority of his family but, Rufus and I just never clicked.

One night after a READY FOR THE WORLD concert we were hanging out at his house in his front yard. I approached him singing. He thought that was the funniest thing. Since his family was full of "Professional" singers, my voice was amateur to him. But it broke the ice and things started shaking up almost right after that.

Flint, MI was a ½ hour drive for me away from my home in Saginaw, MI so I was entertaining a long distance relationship but I didn't care because it felt good. I was not a person who had a lot of boyfriends because my standards were pretty high. Rufus had a jheri curl, but just about everybody did in that day. Rufus was a musician. He wrote and performed with READY FOR THE WORLD as well as his own band. All of that about him was attractive. Sometimes I had to downsize him because his ego was getting out of hand. I had a strong self-confidence about myself at this time as well but his was overwhelming. He thought his career was more important than our relationship.

Whenever I came to town we were always together. Me and Val started to make Flint our second home. Just about every weekend we were there. Our visits was filled with bowling, seeing the band rehearse, carnivals, talent shows, concerts, or just hanging out. We always had a good time. It was a pleasure to be with somebody funny, sensitive, and sentimental with strong family values. I saw us existing for a while but music ruled his life. So I did what I do best, withdraw into my own existence.

Before I left for the military, I came to Flint to say good-bye to Rufus and to see if it was really over. Unfortunately, he was not around. I was hurt but I knew had to go on with my life. Rufus wanted to be a superstar and that fast life while I set it aside for stability. After I settled into my first duty station in Virginia, I received a letter from Rufus saying that he had left the music business alone and joined the military. Needless to say, I was shocked. We wrote all the while why he was in boot camp. His culinary schooling was in Camp Lejeune, North Carolina, only a 3 hour drive from Norfolk, Virginia. We kicked it every weekend. Once again our long distance relationship was thriving. We had gotten so comfortable that we forgot we were in separate branches of the military. He received his stationing orders in Washington D.C. which was a problem.

From 3 hours south to 3 hours north of Norfolk, there was still distance between us. Rufus wasn't going for that. He was ready for commitment. It was actually scary that it happened so fast. We were married in a small chapel in Washington D.C on October 27, 1989, a Friday afternoon. His First Sergeant and Corporal of his unit were our witnesses. Before we went in he said to me "are you sure" I said "yes, of course" then he followed with "because when I get married, it's forever."

We didn't tell his parents. We didn't even have a ring. We left the chapel and went and leased our first apartment because we never lived together. No one wanted to rent to us because they thought we were too young. Our backgrounds overcame all of that. We were both in the military and had good credit. That outweighed any obstacle in our way. We were 21, in love, married, with a 4 month old plan. We were committed. A long distance relationship turned into a marriage and a family. It was a true love story; the kind you see in the movies. Boy meets girl. Boy loses girl. Boy and girl reunite, marry and 23 years later are still together.

ABOUT THE CO-AUTHORS

Rufus and Jenny are one of the very few professional husband and wife teams who do just about everything together, while surviving over twenty years of marriage being attached at the hip.

Rufus Triplett, Jr., originally from Flint, Michigan and a1986 graduate of Flint Northern High School, is a talented singer, songwriter and producer. He co-wrote, produced and toured for the platinum group Ready for the World in the late 80's. He chose to broaden his horizons in the Marine Corps where he went to school for Culinary Arts. After relocating to Atlanta in the early 90's he found a love for computers and has become a technology geek. Not only can he build them from scratch but he has become the "go to" guy for all of his family members. His parents, Rufus Triplett, Sr., a retired firefighter for the City of Flint, and Donzella Triplett, a school teacher for Flint Public Schools, have resided in Flint for over 40 years.

Jenny Triplett, originally from Saginaw, Michigan and a 1986 graduate of Arthur Hill High School, always aspired for a career in media. Starting out as an intern at a 107 FM under DJ Dave Rosas, she established a relationship with several entertainers and Ready for the World where she went on to head their marketing outreach team. Jenny also chose to explore the military where she gained a wealth of knowledge and experience during her time in the United

States Navy. After marrying Rufus and relocating to Atlanta they headed thier own entertainment company w/ the help of Lonell Triplett for over 14 years which included concert promotions and the children's group Kidsworld. Their flourishing company was halted during the time Jenny dealt with legal issue and a brief period of incarceration. The Triplett's do not consider that a dark period in their lives because their marriage grew stronger and they bonded to the point where their relationship became unshakeable. Her parents, Eugene and Mary Jennings are deceased.

The Triplett's now own Dawah International, LLC, a multimedia company, which publishes Prisonworld Magazine and are co-hosts of their own weekly radio show, the Prisonworld Radio Hour which airs on Mondays @ 6pm EST on The Prisonworld Radio Network. They also have a successful blog and are requested speakers for corporate functions, wellness retreats, webinars/teleseminars, correctional facilities, non-profit organizations, schools, colleges and universities, radio shows and print magazines.

Being parents of three boys, Michael, 23, Mosi, 21 and Miles 19, they know the trial and tribulations of not only raising children, but African-American men who could end up as stereotypes. They are passionate about family and detouring young men and women from the criminal justice system. Some of the subjects they speak about are dysfunctional families, substance abuse, entrepreneurship, marriage & relationships, self-conscious addictions, incarceration, stereotypes and the list goes on.

Their appearances on Family Court with Judge Penny and Dr. Phil garnered rave reviews as to their parenting philosophies. Jenny's appearance on The Mike & Juliet Morning show was phenomenal as she gave The Real Housewives of Atlanta a little wisdom. The Triplett's were invited to the Ricki Lake Show as Social Media Influencers, have co-hosted Twitter chats for The Ricki Lake Show (#friendsofricki) and (#dadchat) and carry a KLOUT score of 64. Jenny also contributes to the Daily National and Delux Magazine and has provided comments for CNN, Black Enterprise Magazine, REDBOOK, Ebony Magazine, MSN.com, The Huffington Post, New York Magazine, The LA Times, Reuters, The American Prospect Magazine, Google News, Heart & Soul Magazine, Lagos Times (Nigeria), and a host of other magazine and radio shows.

Mr. & Mrs. Triplett have traveled extensively and seem to draw attention wherever they appear. With their young look and laid back personalities, they are never far from an intelligent conversation. Their creative talents have caused them to branch into television production. The combination of strong story writing and production skills of Jenny and equally as strong songwriting and production skills of Rufus could only be a match made in heaven.

Anyone dealing with inmates has to have a tough demeanor. The Triplett's like to take the non-judgmental and forgiveness approach with their work. Dealing with educating inmates and their families brings great satisfaction to the couple knowing they are a part of improving someone's life. When asked the question what would make you start a magazine like this, the owners respond intelligently "We hope to bring new and different ideas to the multimedia game as well as enlighten views and perceptions of an uninformed and forgotten society." Their constant drive and dedication to thwart mass incarceration was recognized by President Obama.

CONTACT

Rufus & Jenny Triplett

678-233-8286

www.rufusandjennytriplett.com

Man and Wife (the Wedding Song)

Verse1

if I asked you to marry

me would you say yes girl or no

I'm down on 1 knee and begging you

to be my wife and never let go

I'll give all the love that I can give

to you and only you

I made a promise to my lord

to love and honor you

in sickness and in health

till death do us part

as man and wife will be

when we say I do

Chorus

I'm going to marry you

it will be just us 2

and for the rest of my life

I want you as my wife

I'm going to marry you

it will be just us 2

and for the rest of our lives

will be man and wife

Verse2

baby this bond that's between us

I feel it deep down in my soul

so come on and go with me grow with me

together inseparable

I'll give all the love that I can give

to you and only you

I made a promise to my lord

to love and honor you

in sickness and in health

till death do us part

as man and wife will be

when we say I do

Chorus

I'm going to marry you

it will be just us 2

and for the rest of my life

I want you as my wife

I'm going to marry you

it will be just us 2

and for the rest of our lives

will be man and wife

Repeat Chorus:

This song can be heard on the Surviving Marriage Tips website and is available for download.

www.survivingmarriagetips.com

We survived a military marriage-USMC & USN

Rufus & Jenny Triplett Salute Military Marriages that have Survived

Let's face it. The state of marriages in the United States is not something that can be settled strategically in the war room of the pentagon. The days of June and Ward Cleaver are long gone and the days of Cliff and Clair Huxtable are still mostly a TV fantasy.

Finding your soul mate comes along once in a lifetime. Several people have been able to do that under the various branches of military service which exposes you to all parts of the country and various parts of the world. Some have found the military as a sense of security and have reached back for their hometown sweethearts in order to jump the broom.

Even though we met when we were teenagers and still in high school, we married as enlisted personnel in the armed forces. Rufus, was in the United States Marine Corps, and I was in the United States Navy. We saw what seemed to be a domino effect of our fellow service men getting married. Plenty married before us and was asking what was taking us so long to get it done. Some married new loves while others married long time relationships.

64

Military marriages experience more than their share of obstacles. The most unbearing at times is the mandatory deployment for tours of duties which requires the service member to leave spouse and children behind. The separation can go very well or very wrong. It can lead to a deepening strength of affection or it can lead to acts of infidelity. Fortunately and unfortunately we have witnessed both. Fortunately and unfortunately we have seen the survival and demise of both.

It is very possible for two people jump in the foxhole together and fight for happily ever after.

We were fortunate as we never had to experience a deployment due to Rufus' position as a chef for the officers which included the Commandant of the Marine Corps. Our separation due to military orders was limited to field maneuvers and drills and a three week duty station. You could say that I was feeling like the wife of Steven Segal.

We were young and in love and we survived. We were thankful for so much support from so many serving that we knew it was possible. To all who are surviving a marriage involving the military in some shape, form or fashion, WE salute you.

ACKNOWLEDGEMENTS

There is no better time to concentrate on relationships than February. While most are out looking for a special gift to signify a milestone in their relationship, pacify an ongoing relationship, or put a ring on the finger to elevate a relationship, this month will definitely have its fair share of relationship conversations.

In times like these, media does not need to "sugar coat" anything. We have decided this year to dedicate ourselves to bring awareness to marriage and its demise. We have survived a number of trials and tribulations and want to share our experiences with those who may be struggling.

Sending special shout outs and thanks to our children Michael, Mosi & Miles Triplett (very affectionately known as our three grown knuckleheads), our parents, Rufus Sr. & Donzella Triplett, still married and together after 44 years, (Jenny's parents are both deceased), Grandma Triplett (who is 92 years young) our siblings, our 21 nieces and nephews (and the one on the way) our very special neighbor, Ms. Gloria Franklin, and a number of very special friends who have been huge supporters and encouragement along the way. We will not name you all personally because if we forget someone we are sure to be slammed on Facebook and/or Twitter and only celebrities "beef" on social media. So with that said…yall know who you are.

To all of the publishers, freelance writers, magazine staff and publicists who have given input and guidance along the way. Your value and support is most appreciated. To the staff at Ebony Magazine and the Huffington Post, thanks so much. Yall rock!

From Allah we came and to Him we shall return… The Greatest of all

Dawah International, LLC introduces MARRIAGE, the Fragrance that will enhance your life and stimulate your existence. A signature brand and UNISEX SCENT created by Rufus & Jenny Triplett – Ebony Magazine's Couple of the Year 2012

NOW AVAILABLE!!!

www.marriagefragrance.com

(see last page for coupon)

Stay Connected!

http://www.facebook.com/Rufus.JennyTriplett.SurvivingMarriage

Follow us on Twitter @ourmarriagetips

Surviving Marriage Wiz Quiz

Here are 5 Basic Questions, composed by us and based on statistics, to help you gauge where you are with your relationship. This is all in fun. Take it together or take it separately or do both. You can take this quiz on our website (www.survivingmarriagetips.com) to find out how you scored and how you compare to others. If anything, it should spark conversation and maybe help with better communication. Let's Go!

1. **Who do you value most in your life?**
   a. **Your Child/Children**
   b. **Your Parent/Parents**
   c. **Your Girlfriend/Guyfriend**
   d. **Your Spouse**
   e. **God**

2. **How long have you been married?**
   a. **0-5 years**
   b. **6-10 years**
   c. **11-19 years**
   d. **20-25 years**
   e. **25 years & up**

3. **At what age did you first get married?**
   a. **16 - 19**
   b. **20 - 25**
   c. **26 - 30**
   d. **31 – 39**
   e. **40 & up**

4. **When not together, how often do you talk to your spouse daily (including phones calls, emails, text messages, etc?)**
   a. **0**
   b. **1-3**
   c. **4-7**
   d. **8-10**
   e. **Too often to count**

5. **How many times have you disagreed (argued) over money?**
    a. 0
    b. 1-3
    c. 4-7
    d. 8-10
    e. Too often to count

REDEEM THIS COUPON FOR A FREE SAMPLE OF

MARRIAGE – The Fragrance

Send Self Addressed Stamped Envelope to:

Dawah International, LLC

PO Box 380, Powder Springs, GA, 30127

Must be original coupon. No photocopies will be accepted.

Made in the USA
Coppell, TX
31 July 2020